12 SHORT HIKES

IN THE DENVER
FOOTHILLS CENTRAL

TRACY SALCEDO

FALCON®

GUILFORD, CONNECTICUT
AN IMPRINT OF THE GLOBE PEQUOT PRESS

Cover photo by Dennis Thurber
Book design by Jack Atkinson
Overview map by Chalk Butte Inc.
All uncredited photos within the book were taken by Ron Ruhoff, George Meyers and Martin Chourré.

ISBN: 0-934641-81-1

Manufactured in the United States of America
First Edition/Fourth printing

*This book is dedicated to
Gus Bruhl,
in hopes it will inspire and nurture
a love of the outdoors.*

ACKNOWLEDGMENTS

I am forever indebted to the following people, and they know why: the talented folks at Chockstone Press, Ron Ruhoff (and Anna), Dennis Thurber, Sean Hart of Wings of Denver, Ken Foelske and Mark Hearon of the Jefferson County Open Space Department, Susan Werner, Ron Oehklers and Ralph Matzner of the Colorado Division of Wildlife, Angela Logan, Sara and Elliott Bruhl, Carol Hutchings, my parents, Jesse and Cruz, and, most of all, my husband Martin Chourré, whose help and support was invaluable. If I forgot anyone, my apologies. Thank you all.

INTRODUCTION

The centerpiece of this guide is Bear Creek, one of several waterways that flow east from the high country to the South Platte River, and eventually, the Gulf of Mexico. This mellow stream runs through some of the most spectacular country in the foothills west of Denver – most notably, the alpine environs of 14,000-foot Mount Evans. Not every hike is by the water, but the peaceful atmosphere of Bear Creek reaches far beyond its banks. You'll feel its magic in popular Elk Meadow, beneath the smooth rocks of the Three Sisters, in the shadow of the chimney rises from the meadow beyond Groundhog Flat.

The stream meanders through several quaint and historic mountain towns. Morrison, known for both its antiques and fine eateries, is at the mouth of scenic Bear Creek Canyon. Beyond tiny Idledale and rustic Kittredge is Evergreen, the heart of the foothills west of Denver. Here, you'll find all the amenities of modern life.

Each hike, while varying in difficulty, terrain and views, has two key features in common. Each is less than two-and-a-half hours in duration, and each is within an hour's drive of the intersection of Interstate 70 and Colorado Highway 470. Bear Creek Canyon, the cradle of Colo. Hwy. 74, is a main thoroughfare just south of I-70. Hikes are presented east to west along Highway 74.

COMPONENTS OF THIS GUIDE

Each hike is described on two facing pages. Following the hike and park names, you'll find a synopsis of trail length, duration, distance from town and total elevation gain and loss. All statistics were gathered from trail maps, USGS topographic maps, and on-site observations; their accuracy is not guaranteed.

Special characteristics of the hike are summarized in a brief passage, which also includes directions on how to get to the trailhead. The elevation chart shows the ups-and-downs of the trail.

On the facing page, you'll find the trail shown on an aerial photograph of the area.

Below the photo, the **Step by Step** guide details what you'll find along the path and how long it will take you to get from one point to another. This section is designed to help the hiker identify and stay on the route, and to note interesting features and views along the trail. It's also a great way to coax along the kids and the more lackadaisical members of your hiking party – the ultimate in "The top's just around the next bend" method of hiking.

A note on the times: They are not gospel. I'm a strong hiker, but I carried one of my toddlers on each trail, which slowed my pace to what I believe would be posted by the average hiker. The times don't include rest or picnic stops and are rounded to the nearest five-minute mark. Each hiker should set his or her own pace. Kids will slow you down, but the trails are ideal for families.

HIKE WISELY

Generally, hiking in the mountains is a safe and fun way to pass the time. Though there are no gurarantees, there is much you can do to help ensure each outing is a safe and enjoyable one. Below, you'll find an abbreviated list of hiking do's and don'ts, but by no means should this be taken as gospel. I encourage all hikers to verse themselves completely in the science of backcountry travel – it's knowledge worth having and it's easy to acquire. Written material on the subject is plentiful and easy to find – just check with the nearest outdoors or sporting goods store.

For Your Health

• Know the basics of first aid, including how to treat bleeding, bites and stings, and fractures, strains or sprains. Few of these hikes are so remote that help can't be reached within a short time, but you'd be wise to carry and know how to use simple supplies, like over-the-counter pain relievers, bandages and ointments. Pack a first-aid kit on each excursion.

• Familiarize yourself with the symptoms of altitude sickness (especially if you are visiting the area from a significantly lesser altitude – like sea level). If you or one of your party exhibits any symptom of this potentially fatal affliction, including headache, nausea and unusual fatigue, head down. The trail will still be there after you've acclimatized.

• Know the symptoms of both cold- and heat-related conditions, including heat stroke and hypothermia. The best way to avoid these afflictions is to wear clothing appropriate to the weather conditions, drink lots of water, eat enough to keep the internal fire properly stoked, and keep a pace that is within your physical limits.

For Your Safety

• Be prepared for the vagaries of Colorado weather. It changes in a heartbeat. The sun can be brutal, so wear sunscreen. Afternoon and evening thunderstorms, while spectacular, harbor a host of potential hazards, including rain, hail and lightning. Know how to protect yourself. And yes, snow may fall even in summer, so be on guard.

Contents

• The mountains are home to an abundance of wildlife, from gentle squirrels to prowling mountains lions, and plant life, from beautiful columbine to pesky poison ivy. It's a beautiful world, but it also can be unpredictable.

To protect yourself and the environment, I offer this advice: Keep your hands to yourself. Don't pick the flowers – leave them for the next hiker to enjoy. Don't feed the squirrels – they're best able to survive when they're self-reliant, and they aren't likely to find Cheetos along the trail when winter comes.

There are ways to deal with the more dangerous critters in the wilds, like mountain lions, bears and rattlesnakes. Many parks post signs describing useful self-defense tactics should you encounter one of these beasties. Familiarize yourself with the proper etiquette.

For Your Comfort

• Whether short and easy or long and strenuous, you'll enjoy each of these hikes much more if you wear good socks and hiking boots.

• Carry a comfortable backpack loaded with ample water or sport drink, snacks and/or a lunch, and extra clothing, including a warm hat, gloves, and a jacket.

• Maps are not necessary, since these trails are short and well-marked, but they are fun to have along.

• Bring whatever goodies interest you, like a camera, a manual to help you identify wildflowers, binoculars, a topographic map that identifies peaks and valleys, or a good novel to curl up with on a warm rock.

Trail Use

• Many of the trails described herein are also used by horseback riders and mountain bikers. Acquaint yourself with proper trail etiquette and be courteous.

Bear Creek Lake Park

Trail Length:
2.5 miles

Drive Time From
1-70/C-470:
10 minutes

Approx. Time:
1 hour

Elevation change:
40 feet

1

The foothills west of Denver, and the high peaks beyond, would be far less enchanting if the high plains didn't stretch away in a thousand miles of flatness to the Mississippi River. The juxtaposition of these wildly different environments is special and rare. This trail wanders through the prairie and riparian ecosystems near Bear Creek Reservoir, never entering the mountains but always in their shadow. The foothills rise abruptly to the west, but a feeling of vastness comes from the plains that open endlessly to the east, beyond the broad grassy dam that catches the waters of both Bear and Turkey Creeks.

A number of activities take place year-round in Bear Creek Lake Park, including fishing, canoeing, horseback-riding and wind-surfing. There is a small fee.

To reach Bear Creek Lake Park, take C-470 south to the Morrison Road/Colorado Hwy. 8 exit (4.5 miles). Turn left, and follow Hwy. 8 a short distance to the park entrance. The trail begins in the second parking area as you drive east into the park.

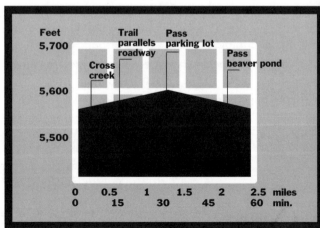

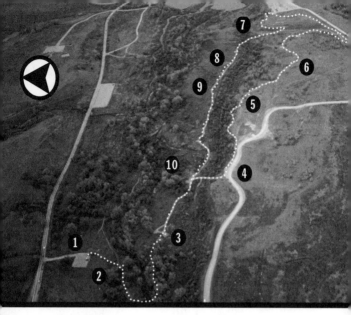

Step By Step

1 Leave the car and walk south toward the creek. Once creekside, head right.

2 Cross the footbridge south over Bear Creek, then head east (left) on the path. (5 min.).

3 Reach the fitness trail. Continue east, crossing a culvert. At the trail fork, go right (southwest) and uphill (10 min.).

4 Crest the hill and follow the trail as it heads east along the dirt road. Shortly, the trail veers away from the road and into the grass. (15 min.).

5 Cross the footbridge and pass an open stand of cottonwoods and elders as well as fitness stop #12) (20 min.).

6 Pass fitness stops #13 and 14. The trail curves south and into an open area before curling back west. Bear Creek Lake lies to the east (25 min.).

7 The trail switches back at fitness stop #16 and heads east toward the lake and its humungous dam. (30 min.).

8 Pass the parking lot and begin a gentle descent to the northeast (35 min.).

9 Head west from the start of the fitness walk, and follow the trail as it gently descends to a lovely meadow and the creek (40 min.).

10 Pass a beaver pond on the right (north). At the intersection, go straight (west) into the circle and pick up the creekside trail. (50 min.).

11 Cross the footbridge and go right (east) back to the parking lot (1 hr.).

"It's the juxtaposition of mountain and prairie that makes this area special."

RED ROCKS/
MORRISON SLIDE LOOP

Red Rocks - Denver Mountain Park
Matthews-Winters Open Space Park

Trail Length:
3.5 miles

Drive Time From
1-70/C-470:
10 minutes

Approx. Time:
1 hour 45 min.

Elevation change:
600 feet

2

The towering, rosy-smooth stone edifices of the Fountain Formation, which make up the ramparts of the famous Red Rocks Amphitheater, are just one remarkable feature of this trail loop. Passing beneath these flaming walls is a moving experience, but so is climbing onto the large, flat plain atop the Morrison Slide. From the summit of this jumble of now-stable rock and soil, which once was part of adjacent Mount Morrison, views open south to the amphitheater and down the hogback valley, east over the hogback to the high plains and north to the Table Mountains. It's a desert up there, studded with yucca and cactus, but enough grass grows in the rocky soil to feed a small herd of deer.

To reach the Red Rocks trailhead, take Interstate 70 west to the Morrison Road exit. Go south (left) on Morrison Road (Colorado Hwy. 26) 1.5 miles to the entrance to Red Rocks Park. Drive up the paved road toward the amphitheater .7 miles to where a dirt road takes off to the left (east). The trailhead is opposite.

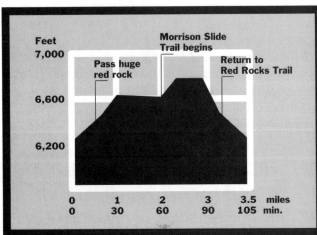

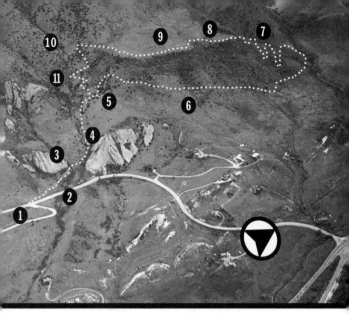

Step By Step

1 Leave the road and walk north up the trail.

2 Pass beneath a tall red rock overhanging a seasonal stream. Shortly, an Open Space sign marks the trail (5 min.).

3 The trail climbs beside a huge red rock formation as it ascends north (10 min.).

4 A rock outcrop rises to the left and above the trail (20 min.).

5 Pass between two junipers as the trail curves to the west (25 min.).

6 Reach the Morrison Slide/Red Rocks trail intersection (30 min.). Go right up a switchback on the Morrison Slide Trail, which meaders north along the face of the slide.

7 Ascend six steep switchbacks that climb up the north face of the slide (50 min.).

8 Pass through lichen-encrusted rocks as you reach the top of the slide (1 hr.).

9 Views, views, views! The trail winds south along the eastern edge of the slide (1 hr. 5 min.).

10 Begin to descend the south face of the slide toward the red rocks (1 hr. 10 min.).

11 Climb down seven steep switchbacks (1 hr. 20 min.).

12 Reach the Red Rocks trail crossing. Proceed south (right and down) on the Red Rocks Trail (1 hr. 25 min.).

13 Pass the Open Space signs as you continue down (1 hr. 35 min.).

14 Finis. (1 hr. 45 min.).

"Pass among flaming rock walls and climb to where the deer have the views."

Lair O' The Bear Open Space Park

Trail Length:
2 miles

Drive Time From
1-70/C-470:
15 min.

Approx. Time:
1 hour

Elevation change:
260 feet

3

In autumn, the cottonwoods, willows and box elders that line the trail through this creekside park erupt in yellows and oranges – a veritable leafy volcano. Looking down from the apex of the Bruin Bluff trail, the color flows like lava in either direction along the shores of Bear Creek. It's quite a sight.

Of course, Lair O' The Bear shines during the rest of the year as well, given the abundant flora and fauna thriving along Bear Creek, the park's centerpiece. This loop allows a visitor to experience it all, from the sparkle of the water rushing under footbridges to the lofty exposure of the rocky bluff, from open meadows of alive with wildflowers to shady stands of pine, fir and aspen. Enjoy.

To reach Lair O' The Bear, take C- 470 south 4.5 miles to the Morrison Road exit (Colo. Hwy. 8). Take Hwy. 8 west through Morrison to the second stoplight. Go straight on Colorado Highway 74, traveling 4.7 miles through scenic Bear Creek Canyon. The park is on the south (left) side of the highway.

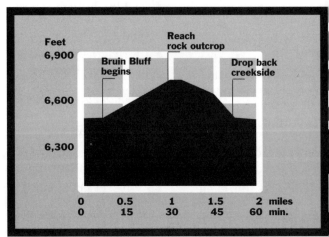

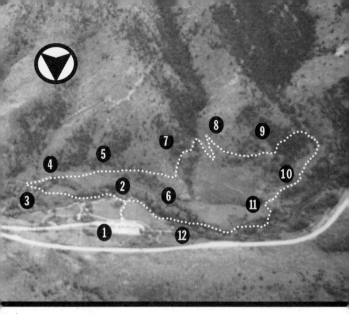

Step By Step

1 From the parking area, go south to the creek on the short access path.

2 Go east (left) on the Creekside Trail. (5 min.).

3 Reach the Bruin Bluff trail at the Ouzel Bridge. Cross the bridge and follow the Bruin Bluff Trail as it gently ascends (10 min.).

4 Reach the Bruin Bluff/Castor Cutoff trail crossing. Go southwest (left), on Bruin Bluff as it rollercoasters along the hillside (15 min.).

5 Climb a steep exposed rocky section, passing two switchbacks (25 min.).

6 Come to the crest of the trail at a rock outcrop that offers lovely views of Bear Creek (30 min.).

7 Pass through an aspen-shaded gully and rest on the bench (35 min.).

8 Climb two switch-backs, then begin to descend back to the creek (40 min.).

9 Wander through a pine glen, dipping into the bed of a seasonal stream, then curve north (45 min.).

10 End the descent in a gully, and follow the creek again (50 min.).

11 Go left at the trail fork, crossing the creek (via the Dipper Bridge) to the Creekside Trail. Go east (right) on the Creekside Trail (55 min.). The Creekside Trail branches right, following the creek beneath a bower of trees.

12 The trail breaks out into the meadow; the parking area is directly north (left). Finis (1 hr.).

"In autumn, the trees that line the trail erupt in yellows and oranges."

Lair O' The Bear Open Space Park

Trail Length:
1.5 miles

Drive Time From
1-70/C-470:
15 minutes

Approx. Time:
45 minutes

Elevation change:
60 feet

4

This route is a fisherman's dream or a mother's nightmare. Ideal for the visitor with limited time, this short loop sticks close to vigorous Bear Creek for the most part, breaking out briefly to wander along the edge of a broad meadow. Much of the path, however, meanders in the shade of the willow, box elder and cottonwood of the riparian zone, where birds, small rodents and reptiles abound. It's a wonderland of discovery for a small child – though bringing a curious youngster along can add hours to the duration of the hike. For the fisherman . . . well, access to the trout in the creek comes at many points. Pick your hole and your degree of solitude – if you can find either on a sunny summer's day.

To reach Lair O' The Bear, take Colorado Highway 470 south 4.5 miles to the Morrison Road exit (Colo. Hwy. 8). Take Hwy. 8 west through Morrison to the second stoplight. Go straight on Colorado Highway 74, traveling 4.7 miles through Bear Creek Canyon. The park is on the south (left) side of the highway.

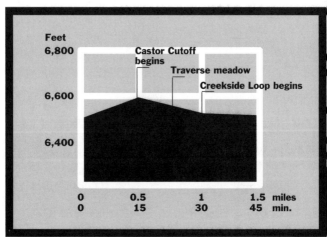

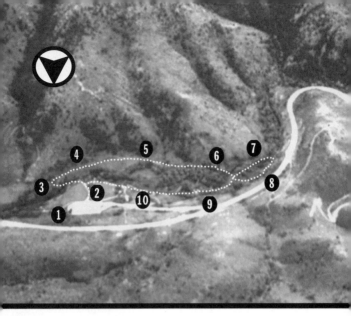

Step By Step

1 From the parking area, go straight south on the access trail to the Creekside Trail.

2 Go east (left) on the Creekside Trail, passing through the lush riparian habitat (5 min.).

3 Reach the Bruin Bluff trail crossing at the Ouzel Bridge. Cross the bridge and follow the Bruin Bluff Trail as it gently ascends (10 min.).

4 Reach the Bruin Bluff/Castor Cutoff trail crossing. Go right on Castor Cutoff, dropping to creekside (15 min.).

5 Walk along the border of a meadow that spreads from the water to the base of the bluff (20 min.).

6 Cross the Dipper Bridge and go north (left) on the Creekside Loop.

Dense willow guards the left side of the trail (25 min.).

7 The trail forks. Go left up the shore of Bear Creek (30 min.).

8 The path loops east away from the creek and circles back to the fork. Continue east (straight) toward the parking area (35 min.).

9 The Creekside Trail branches right, continuing along the shore of the creek and beneath an arbor of trees (40 min.).

10 The trail enters the meadow adjacent to the parking area, which is directly north (to the left). Cross the meadow via the access trail; your chariot awaits (45 min.).

"The path meanders in the shade of willow, box elder and cottonwood."

O'Fallon Denver Mountain Park

 Trail Length:
2.5 miles

 Drive Time From 1-70/C-470:
25 minutes

 Approx. Time:
1 hour 5 min.

 Elevation change:
200 feet

5

Hiking in O'Fallon Park is ideal for the time-pressed loner. The park is rustic, scenic and ramshackle. There are no trail markers, bathrooms or picnic tables, and the trails are maintained by the trampling feet of local hikers, their dogs and the resident wildlife.

Often overlooked by Front Range residents, O'Fallon is never swamped by hikers, even on busy weekends. All the better to enjoy the broad meadow, overgrown with wildflowers in spring, the willow-choked stream that runs trailside for a short distance, and the views of Mount Evans glimpsed through the trees after the rocky climb to the trail's apex.

To reach O'Fallon, take C-470 south to the Morrison Road/Colo. Hwy. 8 exit (4.5 miles). Follow Hwy. 8 west through Morrison, then continue up Bear Creek Canyon on Colo. Hwy. 74. Follow Hwy. 74 for 7.9 miles to the Parmalee Gulch Road in Kittredge; turn left (south) on Parmalee Gulch. Follow the road 1.4 miles to a turnout on the left (east). A chain across a dirt road marks the trailhead.

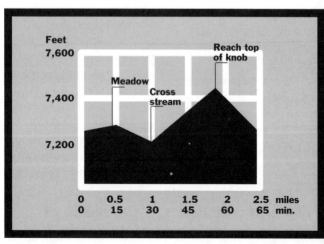

Step By Step

1 Head east, around the gate and up the dirt road.

2 Reach the crest of the hill and a trail intersection. Go east (straight) on the road through a stand of ponderosa pine and begin a short descent (5 min.).

3 Drop into a large meadow and meander southeast through the flowers (10 min.).

4 The road swings around the head of the meadow and drops gently to the north (15 min.).

5 Skirt the willowy creek a short distance and drop into an open gully. At the trail fork, go left (northwest) over the creek (20 min.).

6 Begin to climb (25 min.).

7 Reach the crest of the hill. The roadbed curves to the west (30 min.).

8 Climb a short, steep section (35 min.).

9 The trail flattens as it traverses the top of a grassy knoll. Bear left (north) on the path most traveled (40 min.).

10 Climb to the crest of a wooded hill and keep left (south). The trail continues up along the forested shoulder of a hillside (45 min.). This is a steep, rocky climb, but you're rewarded at the top with . . .

11 . . . A small flat area that offers views west of the snowy flanks of Mount Evans (55 min.).

12 Head downhill to the trail crossing above the meadow. Go right (west) down the road to the pullout (1 hr.).

13 Hop the chain to your car. (1 hr. 5 min.).

"Often overlooked by local residents, O'Fallon is never swamped by hikers."

Foothills to Mount Evans

Upper Bear Creek Road

Buffalo Park Road

Bergen Pe

Brook Forest Road

Evergreen

Bear Cany

Meyers Gulch Road

470

Legend

1. **Fitness Loop,** Bear Creek Lake Park
2. **Red Rocks Trail,** Matthews-Winters Park
3. **Bruin Bluff,** Lair O' The Bear Park
4. **Creekside Loop,** Lair O' The Bear Park
5. **Upper Loop,** O'Fallon Park
6. **Evergreen Lake Trail,** deDisse Park
7. **Ponderosa/Sisters Loop,** Alderfer Park
8. **Evergreen Mountain Loop,** Alderfer Park
9. **Maxwell Falls Trail,** Arapaho National Forest
10. **Meadow View Loop,** Elk Meadow Park
11. **Sleepy S Loop,** Elk Meadow Park
12. **Groundhog Flat,** Arapaho National Forest

Clear Creek Canyon

k

Mount Vernon Canyon

6

70

North and South Table Mountains

reen
ountain

deDisse Denver Mountain Park

 Trail Length:
Approx. 1 mile

 Drive Time From
1-70/C-470:
30 minutes

 Approx. Time:
45 minutes

 Elevation change:
40 feet

6

This lovely man-made lake is the heart of the mountain hamlet of Evergreen. The trail that circles the lake is a mirror of the town itself – it's urban and rural, conventional and unusual, clean and dirty . . . not to mention all wet and dried up.

The beautiful log building at the west end of the lake serves as a warming house for ice skaters in winter and as a boathouse in summer, so you can add water fun to your dry-land adventure if you chose. Any number of happy fisherpeople with loaded stringers can be found around the lake in summer (or sitting around little holes on the ice in winter).

To reach Evergreen Lake, take C-470 south to the Morrison Road/Colo. Hwy. 8 exit (4.5 miles). Follow Hwy. 8 west through Morrison, then continue west on Colo. Hwy. 74, up Bear Creek Canyon. Follow Hwy. 74 10.5 miles to downtown Evergreen. Go through the light and continue on Hwy 74 to Upper Bear Creek Road (11.1 miles). Take a left on Upper Bear, and follow it 0.3 miles to the entrance to Evergreen Lake.

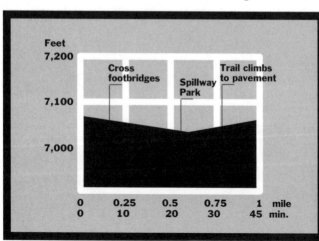

Step By Step

1 Leave the parking lot to the left (northwest) and follow the boardwalk through the wetlands.

2 Cross a footbridge, then go right (east) through willows (5 min.).

3 Cross the second footbridge, then head right (east). (10 min.).

4 After passing a stone wall, the trail forks. Take the upper route, which follows Hwy. 74 to the dam at the east end of the lake (15 min.).

5 Cross the north dam abutment. Go down the stairs, and descend to the park at the foot of the spillway (20 min.).

6 After crossing three footbridges in the spillway park, mount the stairs on the south side of the dam to lakeside. The trail continues west along the south shore of the lake (25 min.).

7 Come to the first of three forks in the trail. Always stay right, at lakeside. The trail climbs to the paved road above (30 min.).

8 Pass a little grey house as the road begins to curve south, away from the lake. A few feet beyond the house, pick up the trail up again. Pass under a pipe, then over a footbridge. At the trail fork, go left (south) and up. (35 min.).

9 The trail runs along the bluff above the lake, then drops down steps to an historic boathouse. Follow the boardwalk back to the large lake house (40 min.).

10 Time to picnic (45 min.).

"This lovely lake is the heart of the mountain hamlet of Evergreen."

Alderfer/Three Sisters Open Space Park

Trail Length:
3.4 miles

Drive Time From
1-70/C-470:
40 minutes

Approx. Time:
1 hour 30 min.

Elevation change:
200 feet

7

Alderfer/Three Sisters is an out-of-the-way gem of a mountain park. The trees are responsible for the marvelous feel of Alderfer – the pines are far enough apart to allow generous sunlight onto the woodland floor, yet close enough to impart a sheltered, protected feel. The Three Sisters, jumbled rock formations that give the park its name, jut above the vanilla-scented ponderosa. Views to the west are of Mount Evans, snowcapped in spring and early summer, muted green and brown in late summer and autumn. To all this, add a quaint farmhouse, a rustic barn and meadows lush with wild iris . . . It's simply perfect.

To reach Alderfer/Three Sisters, take C-470 south to the Morrison Road/Colo. Hwy. 8 exit (4.5 miles). Follow Hwy. 8 west through Morrison, then continue straight on Colo. Hwy. 74 for 10.5 miles to the light in downtown Evergreen. Turn left (south) onto Jefferson County Hwy. 73, going 0.6 miles to the stoplight at Buffalo Park Road. Turn right on Buffalo Park and follow it 2.3 miles to the park's west parking area.

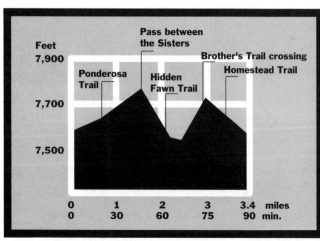

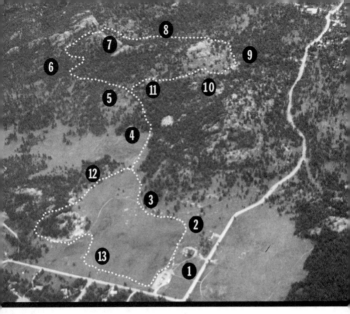

Step By Step

1 Depart north from the parking lot on the Blue-bird Meadow Trail; it curves eastward.

2 Reach the Bluebird Meadow/Silver Fox Trail crossing. Head left (north) on Silver Fox. (5 min.).

3 Reach the first Homestead Trail crossing. Stay on Silver Fox. As the path curves east through meadows, the Sisters come into view (10 min.).

4 Reach the Ponderosa trailhead. Go left (north) on Ponderosa, abandoning meadow for pine and aspen forest (20 min.).

5 Reach the Sisters trailhead. Go left (north) on Sisters Trail (25 min.).

6 Climb 3 switchbacks between the second and third Sisters. (35 min.).

7 Reach the saddle between the two Sisters and descend six rocky switchbacks on the exposed east side of the ridge. (40 min.).

8 Reach the Hidden Fawn trailhead at the base of the ridge. Go right (south) on the Sisters Trail (50 min.).

9 Reach the Ponderosa Trail. Go up left (west) on Ponderosa, climbing three switchbacks (1 hr.).

10 Pass the Brother Lookout Trail. Stay on Ponderosa. (1 hr. 10 min.).

11 Reach the Silver Fox Trail. Take Silver Fox west (1 hr. 15 min.).

12 Reach the Homestead Trail, and follow it around the north side of the rock formation (1 hr. 20 min.).

13 Reach the Bluebird Meadow Trail; follow it to the parking lot (1 hr. 30 min.).

"Alderfer-Three Sisters is an out-of-the-way gem of a mountain park."

Alderfer-Three Sisters Open Space Park

 Trail Length:
4.1 miles

Drive Time From
1-70/C-470:
40 minutes

Approx. Time:
2 hours

Elevation change:
640 feet

8

Compared with Mount Evans, which rises majestically to the west, Evergreen Mountain is but a well-treed nubbin of a foothill – a nubbin well-worth exploring.

A wide, well-maintained trail wanders along the mountain's north face, through a thick lodgepole forest that resounds with silence. The dense canopy of trees is like a green parasol that shelters the forest floor from the bright Colorado sun and insulates the hiker from the surrounding vistas. Still, there are views, east across Evergreen from a prominent rock outcrop, and across a colorful meadow to the striking Three Sisters.

To reach Alderfer/Three Sisters, take C-470 south to the Morrison Road/Colo. Hwy. 8 exit (4.5 miles). Follow Hwy. 8 west through Morrison, then continue straight on Colo. Hwy. 74 for 10.5 miles to the light in downtown Evergreen. Turn left (south) onto Jefferson County Hwy. 73, going 0.6 miles to the stoplight at Buffalo Park Road. Turn right on Buffalo Park and follow it 2.3 miles to the park's west parking area.

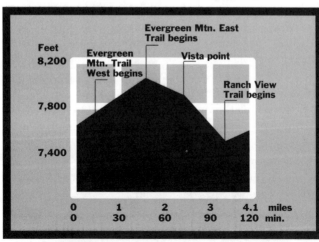

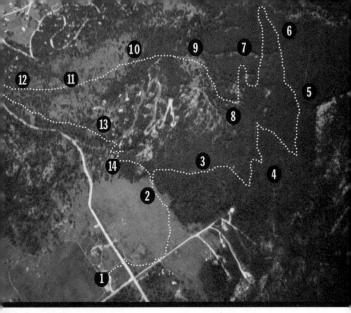

Step By Step

1 Depart the parking lot, crossing Buffalo Park Road to the south meadow. Take a right on the Wild Iris Loop.

2 Reach the Evergreen Mtn. West Trail crossing. Go southwest (right) on Evergreen Mtn. West (10 min.).

3 Follow the trail as it climbs west through the trees. Cross a shallow gully. The trail rounds a switchback, then crosses another gully (25 min.).

4 Climb four switch-backs and continue gently upward (40 min.).

5 Reach the inter-section of the Evergreen Mtn West, Evergreen Mtn. East and Summit Trails. Go east (left) and down on the Evergreen Mtn. East Trail (50 min.).

6 Reach a rock over-look. The trail switches back west (1 hr.).

7 Cross a gully and head east through a grassy open area (1 hr. 5 min.).

8 The trail passes beneath a large rock (1 hr. 10 min.).

9 Switch back west into the trees (1 hr. 15 min.).

10 Descend yet another switchback, then head north across an open slope (1 hr. 20 min.).

11 The trail flattens and meanders through lovely meadow and an aspen grove (1 hr. 25 min.).

12 Reach the Ranch View Trail. Go west (left) on Ranch View (1 hr. 35 min.).

13 Cross a paved road and hike four switchbacks (1 hr. 45 min.).

14 Reach the Wild Iris Loop Trail. Go right (1 hr. 50 min.).

15 Collapse at the car (2 hrs.).

Arapaho National Forest

 Trail Length:
Approx. 3 miles

 Drive Time From
1-70/C-470:
45 minutes

 Approx. Time:
1 hour 20 min.

 Elevation change:
520 feet

9

These peaceful falls are tucked back in a quiet drainage in the Arapaho National Forest. The water cascades year-round – in spring the pools are full and water spills vigorously down the rocks; in autumn, the stream moves slowly, trickling from basin to basin.

The gentle trail wanders along Maxwell Creek through ponderosa and lodgepole forest, punctuated by the occasional small aspen grove. The trail forks near the falls; the main trail leads to a shady picnic/rest spot perched atop the falls. The smaller footpath follows Maxwell Creek to the base of the falls, where, in spring, the mist and the noise are invigorating.

To reach Maxwell Falls, take C-470 south to the Morrison Road/Colo. Hwy. 8 exit (4.5 miles). Follow Hwy. 8 through Morrison, then go west on Colo. Hwy. 74 for 10.5 miles to the light in downtown Evergreen. Turn left (south) onto Jefferson County Hwy. 73, driving 1 mile to Brook Forest Road. Follow Brook Forest 4.3 miles to the dam at Stevenson Reservoir. Parking is at the foot of the dam.

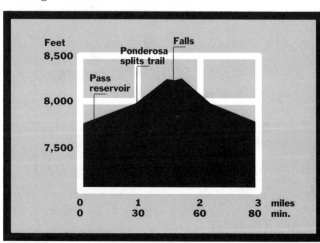

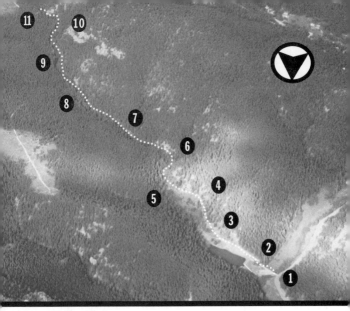

Step By Step

1 Leave the parking lot and climb up the road on the right (west) side of the dam.

2 Beyond the reservoir, the path narrows to a trail that heads south through meadow and aspen (5 min.).

3 The trail climbs a bit, then levels out in a meadow (10 min.).

4 Descend into a gully. Maxwell Creek comes into view (15 min.).

5 Cross a seasonal stream and begin to climb into the forest (20 min.).

6 The trail levels out in an open area, then begins to climb again (25 min.).

7 A ponderosa splits the trail at a rock outcrop overlooking the creek. The trail drops, then levels out and rambles creekside (30 min.).

8 Begin to climb again. Pass a large rock outcrop on the west (35 min.).

9 The trail forks. The main trail ascends to the right (west); the less-traveled path leads to the base of the falls (a five-minute jaunt) (40 min.).

10 Climb two switch-backs to the crest of the trail above the falls. (45 min.).

11 Descend two switch-backs to the creek, which is crossed via a path that breaks away to the left (south) before the main trail begins to climb again (50 min.).

12 After exploring the falls, retrace your steps back to the trailhead. The return takes about 30 minutes, since it's all downhill to the reservoir (1 hr. 20 min.).

"These falls flow vigorously in spring, and trickle from basin to basin in fall."

MEADOW VIEW/ PAINTER'S PAUSE LOOP

Elk Meadow Open Space Park

Trail Length:
4.5 miles

Drive Time From
1-70/C-470:
30 minutes

Approx. Time:
2 hours

Elevation change:
300 feet

10

Pleasant and relatively flat, this hike meanders through the meadow and forest that blanket the eastern flank of 9,708-foot Bergen Peak. The huge meadow is chameleon-like – in spring its vibrant green is painted with swaths of yellow, pink and purple wildflowers; in fall, the golden grasses are stained with russet, red and orange. The relatively open stands of lodgepole and ponderosa pine are dotted with aspen. Oh ye who would get away from all signs of civilization, don't despair – the sounds of the nearby highway eventually fade as you hike into the forest.

Elk Meadow Park, one of the most popular in the foothills, offers a variety of hiking opportunities. If you really want to wear yourself out, head to the top of Bergen Peak via the Too Long Trail and the Bergen Peak Trail (this will take the better part of a day).

To reach Elk Meadow, take Interstate 70 west 8.5 miles to the Evergreen Parkway exit (Exit 252). Follow Colo. Hwy. 74 south to the stoplight at Lewis Ridge Road. Turn right (west) at the light, and park in the large lot on the west side of Hwy. 74.

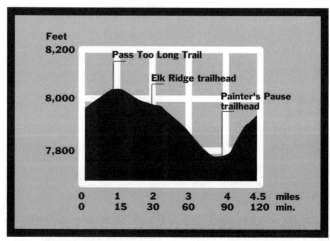

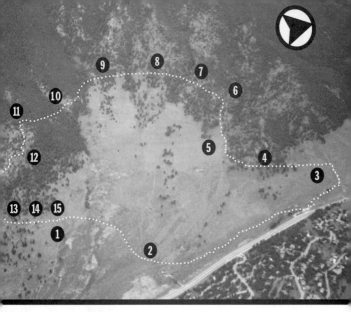

Step By Step

1 A spur trail takes you from the parking lot to the Sleepy S Trail. Go east (right) on Sleepy S to the Painter's Pause Trail, which heads north and gradually uphill through the meadow.

2 Painter's Pause crosses the service road to the barn. (10 min.).

3 Reach Meadow View Trail intersection. Go west on Meadow View (35 min.).

4 Reach the top of a grade; the trail narrows (50 min.).

5 Pass a fence on the left and a bird feeder on right (north). Begin a gentle ascent (55 min.).

6 Pass two switchbacks, then the trail heads south through the woods along the eastern flank of Bergen Peak (1 hr.).

7 Pass the Too Long Trail trailhead (1 hr. 5 min.).

8 Drop into first of five dips in the trail. A small rock grotto shadows the trail (1 hr. 10 min.).

9 Third dip: the trail passes through an aspen grove and crosses a small bridge (1 hr. 20 min.).

10 Fifth dip (1 hr. 30 min.).

11 Reach the Elk Ridge trailhead. Go left (east) on the exposed, rocky trail. (1 hr. 35 min.).

12 Trail steepens and winds down switchbacks as it drops to the meadow (1 hr. 45 min.).

13 Reach the intersection of Elk Ridge and Sleepy S Trails. Head left (east) on Sleepy S through the meadow (1 hr. 50 min.).

14 Reach the intersection with the spur trail back to the parking lot (1 hr. 55 min.).

15 Home (2 hr.).

Elk Meadow Open Space Park

Trail Length:
2.5 miles

Drive Time From
I-70/C-470:
35 minutes

Approx. Time:
1 hour

Elevation change:
320 feet

11

The open parkland of ponderosa pine at the tail end of this hike is a wonderfully beautiful and peaceful place.

Though the views are spectacular and the brief dip into the meadow is nice, the gentle forest is the highlight of this walk. In the moist shade of the ponderosa, the purple Pentstemon and bright paintbrush grow lush in spring – you may even see a delicate wild iris. The sights and sounds of civilization have yet to intrude here, so you can fully enjoy the sheltered and diverse forest habitat.

Though this loop is shorter than its brethren hikes within Elk Meadow Park, this jaunt offers relatively challenging ascents and descents. Bring along your hiking shoes and some energy.

To reach Elk Meadow, take Interstate 70 west 8.5 miles to the Evergreen Parkway exit (Exit 252). Take Colorado Highway 74 south through Bergen Park. Follow Hwy. 74 for 5.3 miles to its intersection with Stagecoach Blvd. Turn right and follow Stagecoach Blvd. 1.2 miles west to the Elk Meadow parking area.

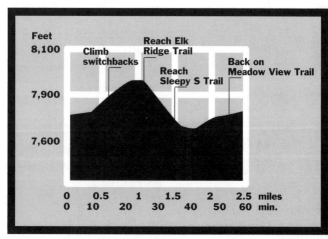

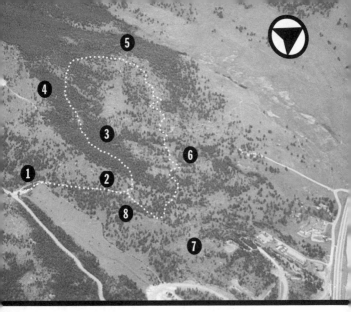

Step By Step

1 Leave the parking area and follow the Meadow View Trail as it climbs gently to the northeast (right).

2 Reach the first Sleepy S Trail intersection. Continue northeast (left) on Meadow View, which meanders through dense evergreen and aspen stands (5 min).

3 Pass two switchbacks (15 min.).

4 Pass the Bergen Peak trailhead. Continue north (right) on the Meadow View Trail (20 min.).

5 Reach the Elk Ridge Trail crossing. From here, you can enjoy views east to the high plains (25 min.). Go east on the Elk Ridge Trail, cresting the ridge, then descending several switchbacks into the meadow.

6 Once in the grassland, you'll reach the intersection of the Sleepy S and Elk Ridge Trails. Head southwest (right) on the Sleepy S Trail, enjoying the brief sojourn through the openness before gently ascending into the ponderosa stands (35 min.).

7 The trail climbs, sometimes steeply, to the west through the widely spaced ponderosas. Pass a bench on the left side of the well-maintained path (50 min.).

8 Reach the intersection of the Meadow View and Sleepy S trails (passed much earlier in the hike). Go west (left) on the Meadow View Trail (55 min.).

9 Return to the parking area (1 hr.).

"The open parkland of ponderosa pine is a wonderfully peaceful place."

GRASS CREEK TRAIL/ GROUNDHOG FLAT

Arapaho National Forest

Trail Length:
4.5 miles

Drive Time From
1-70/C-470:
50 minutes

Approx. Time:
1 hr. 45 min.

Elevation change:
400 feet

12

Groundhog Flat is "out there." High on the eastern flanks of Mount Evans, this is a hike on the wild side, offering few signs of civilization and abundant alpine scenery. The hike follows Grass Creek to a broad meadow in the shadow of the tundra-covered summit of 14,258-foot Mount Evans. Along the trail you'll pass the staples of mountain hiking – ancient stands of aspen, ponderosa glades and several spectacular vista points. At trail's end, you can eat lunch in what is left of an old homestead. Savor the seclusion – you'll never feel so alone this close to civilization.

To reach the trailhead, take C-470 south to the Morrison Road/Colo. Hwy. 8 exit (4.5 miles). Follow Hwy. 8 west through Morrison, then continue on Colo. Hwy. 74 10.5 miles to Evergreen, then 0.6 miles to Upper Bear Creek Road. Turn left, and follow Upper Bear 6.4 miles, where the road forks. Go right on the dirt County Road 481 for 2 miles to a fork with a sign for the elk management area. Go left, clinbing 1 mile to the wildlife area gate and then 0.7 miles to the small parking lot.

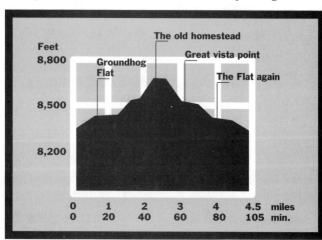

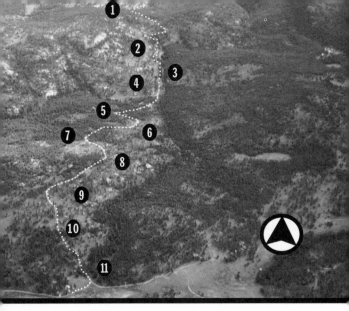

Step By Step

1 From the parking lot, head south (left) on the fire road. Pass a gate and begin to climb.

2 Crest the hill; the trail passes through an aspen grove before heading down (5 min.).

3 Reach the bottom of the hill and wander streamside through large ponderosas (10 min.).

4 Pass picnic tables on the left (southeast), then a sign describing controlled fires. There's a nice rock formation on the left (east) side of the creek (15 min.).

5 Cross the bridge and start uphill (20 min.).

6 About halfway up the hill, pass a sign that describes dwarf mistletoe (25 min.).

7 As you continue up, the road enters an open area, with nice views to the southeast of the forested hills. Stroll through some aspen groves, passing a side road on the left (30 min.).

8 Pass a harvest sign in an aspen grove (35 min.).

9 Crest another hill, passing a striking rock formation on the left , yet another sign describing prescribed burns and an old stand of aspen. Begin a gentle descent (45 min.).

10 Pass a sign describing Abert squirrels and continue through a flat, wooded area (50 min.).

11 Picnic in the meadow. The homestead is in the northwestern corner of the intersection (55 min.).

12 Return the way you came – this'll take the same amount of time, as the trail is more a roller-coaster than an up-and-down affair (1 hr. 45 min.).

"Savor the solitude – you'll never feel so alone this close to civilization."

OTHER BOOKS
IN THE SHORT HIKES SERIES

DENVER AREA:
12 Short Hikes: Boulder
12 Short Hikes: Denver Foothills North
12 Short Hikes: Denver Foothills South

COLORADO MOUNTAINS:
12 Short Hikes: Aspen
12 Short Hikes: Steamboat Springs
12 Short Hikes: Summit County
12 Short Hikes: Vail

About The Author

photo by Elliott Bruhl

Tracy Salcedo has lived in Evergreen, Colorado, for ten years. She worked as a reporter and associate editor for a Colorado weekly newspaper and has published articles in *Mountain Bike* magazine and *San Francisco* magazine. She currently edits and assembles guidebooks for Chockstone Press, and writes a column on the outdoors for a local newspaper. She hikes, skis and bikes as often as her husband and twin sons allow.

Address all comments, additions or correction to the author, in care of The Globe Pequot Press, P.O. Box 480, Guilford, Connecticut. Orders for this or other books in this series may be made by writing to the above address.